Kanha Priya

Romantic Moments in Poetry and Painting

Kanha Priya

Romantic Moments in Poetry and Painting

Harsha V. Dehejia
Vijay Sharma

ARYAN BOOKS INTERNATIONAL
New Delhi

ISBN: 978-81-7305-353-5

Designed by Phil D'Costa, Ottawa, Canada
Processed by Reproscan, Mumbai, India

First published in 2009 by
ARYAN BOOKS INTERNATIONAL
Pooja Apartments, 4B, Ansari Road, New Delhi - 110 002 (India)
Telephone: +91-11-23287589, 23255799; Facsimile: +91-11-23270385
E-mail: aryanbooks@vsnl.com; aryanbooks@gmail.com

KANHAPRIYA

A Journey from Kavya to Kalam

The giant and majestic tree of miniature paintings of *shringara rasa* has its roots in *kavya* or poetry, and throughout its evolution and through its many artistic representations, it has been nourished by these roots and maintains a strongly poetic ambience and not only *chitra* but equally *shilpa and natya* remain in the end visual poetry

Kavya or poetry is the key to the many colours and nuances, form and feelings of *shringara rasa,* and it alone is able to combine the cosmic dimensions of myth and the sensuality of the throbbing heart, the variegated colours of longing and belonging, the joy of anticipation and the pain of separation, the red of passionate love and the yellow of the first mango blossoms of spring, of the cry of the *chakravaka* as it longs for its mate and of the longing of the *chataka* as it waits for the drop of rain, and therefore it is only appropriate that the flute of Krishna and the foot falls of the *gopis* be heard first in poetry and then expressed in the various arts and particularly in miniature paintings.

Shringara rasa kavya falls under the rubric of *khandiata kavya*, or fragmented poetry, as opposed to *maha kavya* or epic poetry, and uses words charged with suggestion and metaphors, and has an aural texture that evokes vivid mental images and is therefore able to convey in a few words the fully animated, beautiful and energised and charged romantic moment between the lover and the beloved. There is about this form of romantic poetry a spontaneity and earthiness, it expresses a joy of sensual pleasures, in this poetry there are no major plots or epic stories, it does not concern itself with gods and goddesses, there is no moralising and no lofty metaphysics, just the immediacy and the thrill of that romantically charged passionate moment. That romantic moment is tied to and resonates with the world of nature, the sap that flows through the *nayika* and the *nayaka* in the *kavyas* is no different from that which animates the birds and the trees, there are no mansions or palaces, no regal pretense, no pomp or ceremony, but just the heart throb of love and of the excitement of pulsating desire and of the many situations in which two people lived and loved and found each other.

The ethos of romantic poetry for us in the Indian tradition is pre-historic. The Halasapta and the Aham poetry of the Tamil Sangam literature are the first extant collections of romantic poetry. It is noteworthy that this poetry was not in Sanskrit, clearly signaling that while Sanskrit was the language of philosophical discourse and court proceedings, it did not concern itself with matters of the heart early in the tradition. Amarau's Shataka and Bhartrhari's Shringara Trayi were early compositions in romantic poetry in Sanskrit. There is enough evidence to suggest that the 9th-10th century Bhagavata Purana was the first Sanskrit text to enunciate an emotional devotion to Krishna. It was composed in the Tamil country, perhaps in the Pandya region, and it attained the status of a major Purana very quickly. The popularity of the Purana, not only in the south but all across the continent, is due in no small measure to the richly romantic ambience that pervades in the *dashama skanda*, the tenth book of the Purana, for it was for the first time that a religion of ecstasy based on romantic love was given Puranic legitimacy. Pre-Islamic India of 10th century was now ready to receive a religion that harmonised the intellectuality and transcendence of the northern Vedanta, the emotional fervour of the south as seen in the Sangam literature along with the spontaneity and earthiness of a popular or tribal erolticism and all this was to be found in the Bhagavata Purana. This was no easy task for the Bhagavata, through its simple songs and stories retains the *advaita* of Vedanta along with *dvaita* of the Alvars and the folk religion and in doing so forges a unique form of *advaita,* called *shuddha advaita*. While the Alvars recognised *maya* (Tamil *mayam, mayai*) this was very different from the *maya* of Shankara.

Maya for the Alvars were the miraculous and elusive exploits of the mischievous and romantic Krishna. The Bhagavata was able to reconcile these conflicting concepts through the twin epistemology of *madhurya* and *viraha* both of which were the corner stones of the *shringara rasa* of Krishna.

Once the romantically charged space of the *shringara rasa* of Krishna and the *gopis* was created in the *dashama skanda* of the Bhagavata Purana it led to many journeys for *bhaktas* and *rasikas* alike. Krishna *bhakti* was to take on an aesthetic texture and move away from religious rites and sacred rituals. The lifting of the Govardhana was Krishna's signal to move away from onerous Vedic ceremonies to a more emotional engagement with the divine and Indra's prostration to Krishna is a clear indication that even though the authority of the Vedas was not questioned the *karma kanda* or the many rituals were in the decline. The Bhagavata Purana clearly states:

shradhhalur mat kathah shravan su bhadra loka pavanih
gayan anusmaran karma janma cha abhinayan muhuh.
Listening to my stories with faith and singing
and remembering and enacting my deeds and incarnations
purifies the world.
11.11.23

The Bhagavata thus clearly establishes an aesthetic, rather than a ritualistic celebration and veneration of Krishna. The preferred mode of veneration was *kirtana* or the communal singing rather than just recitation. While this remains the staple of Vaishnava theology and was the modus operandi of the *bhakti* movement, what the *rishis* of the Bhagavata and even Jayadeva did not realise was that within five hundred years of the Bhagavata, not just *kavya* or poetry but *chitra* or painting was to become an equally important and evocative vehicle of the celebration of the *shringara bhakti* of Krishna.

The Bhagavata is very clear about the public celebration of Krishna when it describes the ways in which it done:

maj janma karma kathanam mama parvanumodanam
gita tandava vaditra goshtibhit mad grhotsavah
Reciting pleasing stories of me and my incarnations and deeds
celebrating festivals in my temple with song
dance, music and discourses.
Bhagavata Purana 11.11.36

The importance of this last statement in the Bhagavata cannot be over emphasised for it legitimises the use of the *bhashas* in the celebration of Krishna and thus it is that *brajbhasha* in western India, and *brajboli* or Bengali in eastern India, became the main vehicles of Krishna's lore of *shringara rasa* in medieval India. The five or six hundred years that followed the Bhagavata, till the *pushtimarg sampradaya* was established by Vallabhacharya in Nathadwara, saw the evolution and transformation of the *gopi geet* in Sanskrit to *haveli sangeet* in the *bhashas*. While Sanskrit, through its majestic and magisterial words and tone, is irreplaceable when it comes to the intellectual side of Krishna's deeds, the various shades of Krishna's *shringara rasa* are best conveyed by the earthy and sweet words of the *bhashas*. The preference given to local languages resulted in rich traditions of Vaishnava devotional literature in these languages. When it comes to

miniature painting it is Krishna poetry in *braj bhasha*, and not so much *braj boli* in Bengali, that was to play a dominant role. And it was none other than Surdas and the *ashtachap kavis* of the *pushtimarg* tradition at Nathadwara that inaugurated heart throbbing and warmly evocative Krishna poetry in the *bhashas*. It were these richly effusive and disarmingly direct love songs of Krishna that became the cornerstone of *haveli sangeet*, that was not only performed in Vaishnava temples and courts of the Vaishnava Rajputs, but was equally sung in the fields and streets by ordinary people and is performed even today. *Haveli sangeet* is richly endearing, what it lacks in classical refinement it more than makes up in its appeal to the heart. Through its simple lyrics in the language of the people, and melody appropriate to the romantic mood, it brings the love of Radha and Krishna to the people, and because of this Krishna does not remain a distant god but becomes a part of our daily lives, available to us through the joys and sorrows of our earthly life. In the *dashama skanda* we find this verse:

kacit samam mukendena svara jatir amisritah
unninye pujita tena proyata sadhu sadhv iti
Bhagavata Purana, 10.33.10
Krishna praised the gopis even though they sang in a different pitch.

The *gopis* sang of their love for Krishna and even though the songs were not technically perfect Krishna praised them, for Krishna, according to the Bhagavata, was touched by the loving devotion of the *gopis* and not the musical perfection in those songs. This underscores the importance of emotional sincerity and not intellectual propriety in *shringara bhakti* and music according to the Bhagavata is the perfect vehicle for this. While this statement of the Bhagavata presages the growth of various love songs in the *bhashas* over the next several hundred years the *rishis* of the Bhagavata may not have realised that it is this very *kavya* and *sangeet* that would be transformed into the most evocative miniature paintings over five hundred years and would become a visual representation of that very touching and endearing *shringara bhakti*. The artists of the Rajput ateliers, who may not have been well versed in the minutiae of the Bhagavata as a text, and who may not have had intellectual erudition or finesse, could not but have been influenced by the performance of *haveli sangeet,* and their *kalam* must have responded not only to the demands of the pictorial composition and the requirement of the patron, but also and more importantly to the sounds and rhythms of this *sangeet*. For it has been rightly said that if the words of the Bhagavata speak of Krishna's deeds the music of the Bhagavata reveals Krishna's spirit, which was one of evocation of *shringara rasa* in all its richness and dimensions not only to the *gopis* but to all of Vrindavana, both animate and inanimate.

The next major step in the evolution of the poetry of *shringar bhakti* was Jayadeva's Gita Govinda, which was not only the acme of classical romantic Sanskrit poetry but marked a milestone in the history of *shringara bhakti,* the emotional celebration of the romantic Krishna. Jayadeva humanises Krishna and makes Radha occupy the centre stage of romantic love. Kapila Vatsyayan states that "Radha Astands in a one to one relationship with Krishna whether jealous or impetuous, forbidding or captivating, she is the woman in love, separation and union. None of the nascent sketches of (her) character in previous literature provides us with a predecessor. Jayadeva fills every limb of the character (of Radha) with sap, rich and sensuous, but human and endearing." Equally importantly Jayadeva creates a special place for the *sakhi*. Clearly an outgrowth of the *gopis* of the Bhagavata the *sakhi*, as the friend and go-between of Radha and Krishna, becomes central in Gaudiya or Bengal Vaishnavism and assumes an epistemological importance in the hands of Chaitanya. What is important to note is how quickly the Gita Govinda spread across the country. It is likely that it may have been taken to Nepal soon after its creation but within half a century it had reached western India and was already a part of the ritual of Vaishnava temples as is evident from the Patan inscription of 1295 CE. The Gita Govinda very soon transformed itself from a poetic text into a performing art as it was sung and danced in village squares and temples including the Jaggannatha temple at Puri, a tradition that still continues. The Gita Govinda transformed itself into two streams: a ritual text for the Chaitanya Vaishnavas and a performance text for dancers and painters.

In the centuries after Jayadeva there were two major movements in the country, the *bhakti* cult which swept across most of north India and produced its own genre of poetry in the hands of singer saints such as Tulsidas

and Mira, but in the field of romantic poetry it was the period of *riti kavya.* The Radha Krishna model of romantic love which arose in the Bhagvata Purana and which was brought to a climax by Jayadeva in classical Sanskrit now moved on to the *bhashas* and was expressed especially in Hindi and its dialects. The aesthetic space of romantic love was already created and *riti kavya* celebrates that love as it moves fluidly between religious devotion and urbane romanticism and Krishna is humanised. The *riti kala* poets embraced the romantic love of Radha and Krishna and north India resonated with their beautiful compositions, and the love of Radha and Krishna moved from the mythic Vrindavana to the courts and the *havelis* of the Rajput kings and took on yet another dimension.

It is important to recognise two different strands in Radha Krishna poetry of medieval India. While *riti kavya* celebrated the romantic love of Radha and Krishna in sensuous and secular terms and set it in a courtly ambience and provided a number of beautiful situations for the painters, *bhakti kavya* on the other hand was entirely devotional in character. While recognising this difference, one hastens to point out that *riti kavya* also transcends sensuality towards spirituality and *bhakti kavya* in being religious does not negate the earthly and the romantic, and therefore in a sense these two distinct poetic expressions must be considered two fibres of the same fabric of Radha Krishna lore, or two streams in the river of romantic love. However it would be fair to say that the audiences for each genre of poetry were different and it was *riti kavya* that was to be become the main inspiration for miniature paintings in the 17th and 18th centuries.

Ritikavya breaks new ground in humanising Krishna and converting him into a secular *nayaka* from a divine cowherd. While *bhakti kavya* celebrated the divinity of Krishna in homes and *havelis* and at religious gatherings in temples and home shrines, there was another equally strong current of evocative poetry and that was *ritikavya* which resonated in courts. These were the Rajput courts in northwest India and the Himalayan kingdoms where Krishna's presence was that of a *nayaka* or a romantic hero, as this suited the ambience of the courts and the patronage of the kings. And as Krishna is transformed into a *nayaka*, a secular romantic hero, and the kings identified with that image, the *gopis* then became the *nayikas* or romantic and courtly heroines and *ritikavya* took its stand on the many interactions between the *nayaka* and the *nayika,* and the genre of *nayaka-nayika- bheda* became an important part of *ritikavya* and of miniature paintings that were to emerge from the Rajput courts of that period.

The *ashtanayikas* of Bharata had already been enunciated many centuries back in the Natyashastra but these were limited to eight and not sufficient for the *ritikal* poets and they expanded it to many more so that it could include the intrigue and emotions, the fears and anxiety, the coyness and peevishness of the courtly Radha in her amorous relationships with an equally courtly Krishna. She was no longer the rustic *gopi* of Vrindavana but the mature lover, accomplished in the many nuances and arts of love, sometimes demanding and at other times aggressive, exercising her rights and even forcing Krishna to submission. She is *chatrini, padmini* and *shankhini, mugdha* and *praudhamana* and *svadhinapatika* and many more. *Ritikal* poets did not leave any romantic situation and any nuance of love untouched in their creations, they painted every hue of her longing, every colour of her belonging, they captured every texture of her mood and every meaning of her gesture in their poetry. Radha and Krishna in the hands of the *ritikal* poets were a courtly pair of lover and beloved, elegant and urbane, with finesse and grace and who carried romantic love to its limits of aesthetic sophistication. In creating the many *nayikas ritikavya* incorporated the enunciations of Bharata in his Natyashastra, the nuances of the *nagarika* or the cultured elite in Vatsyayan's Kama Sutra, Kalidas' cultured heroines from his *mahakavyas*, the accomplished woman of Bhartrhari in his Ṣhataka Trayi and Amarushataka, the graceful Radha of Jayadeva and the many romantic poets that came later, but at no time was the pastoral *gopi* of the Bhagavata lost sight of. The self-effacing and sweet love of the *gopis* for Krishna remained like an undercurrent at all times even when creating the many romantic situations of the courtly Radha in *ritikavya*.

Ritikal poets were *rasikas* in the true sense for they had a deep emotional response to beauty, not only of human beauty but of beauty in everything around them, in the strains of music or the song of a bird, the whisper of a blossom and the evocative suggestiveness of a creeper winding around the trunk of a tree and they related all this to romantic love. Beauty and love in the hands of the *ritikal* poets were intertwined as one reinforced the other and one was incomplete without the other and this in no small measure provided the miniature artists the inspiration to create the courtly ambience and the luxuriant landscape. *Ritikal* poets ensured that even in the courtly and regal atmosphere of the Rajput courts the *shringara rasa* of Krishna was not lost, that it was always central in the worship of Krishna, that neither political intrigue nor the overpowering Mughal influence was to overshadow it.

Two names among many others stand out in the genre of *ritikavya* and those are of Keshavdas and Bihari. Keshavdas created the monumental Rasikapriya which is considered a *lakshana granth*, a reference manual, of endless *nayikas* in numerous romantic situations, depicting every possible mind-set of the woman in love, for whom there was no greater purpose than indulging and celebrating love as an end in itself, pulsating with many and varied romantic encounters that brought out the depth and the sincerity of love. Keshavdas is a poet's poet and remained like a sentinel from whom other poets of the *ritikal* drew inspiration and remains one of the most illustrated poets in the miniature tradition of Rajasthan and the Pahari region. Bihari was another significant *ritikal* poet who in his Satsai makes the *nayika* come alive in a rainbow of amorous colours and a kaleidoscope of romantic situations. It is said of Bihari that through the well sculpted words of his gem like *dohas* he created sparkling romantic situations in which the *nayaka* and the *nayika* shone as they radiantly expressed their love in a courtly setting:

satsai ke dohare jyon shavak ke teer
dekhan mai chhote lagae ghaav gambhir.
The couplets of the Satsai may appear insignificant but
inflict a deep wound like the arrow of a hunter.

Ritikal was a richly fertile period and the genre of *ritikavya* produced many poets who followed in the footsteps of Keshavdas and created charming *shringara rasa kavyas*. Names such as Matiram, Ghanananda, Puhakar, Bhagwan, Sunder and Gwal among others come to mind. Their gem like creations, although in the shadow of Keshavdas' Rasikapriya, still shine and speak, not only of their personal accomplishments as poets but also of the sparkling period of *ritikal* where the celebration of love through the various arts was a cherished activity especially in courts and in cultured and cultivated company of *rasikas*.

The poetry and paintings of the Bhagavata, Gita Govinda, Surdas, Rasikapriya and Sat Sai remain the primary source and the gold standard of the artistic representations of *shringara rasa* of Krishna and these have a timeless presence in museums and private collections, in books and in catalogues. These paintings remain the most important documents of *shringara rasa* paintings and will continue to inspire and beckon *rasikas* of Krishna for generations to come. However there are contemporary poets and painters, who having been touched by these classic compositions and who are soaked in the colours and hues of Krishna's *shringara rasa*, and who are inspired to create new compositions and to celebrate the timeless love of Krishna. In doing so these poets and painters are creating new art but are not distancing themselves from the long and hoary pedigree of master poets and artists that have come before them, and through their creations they are continuing the beautiful tradition of *shringara rasa kavya* and *chitra*. Their art therefore can be considered neo-classical. Even though

the compositions may be new the motifs and metaphors, the technique and texture, the forms and the faces are drawn from the rich treasures of the past centuries. To be touched by the ancient and re-create Krishna's *shringara rasa* is a tribute to ancient creators who have left behind timeless and enduring creations. Newer poets and painters are not content to luxuriate in beautiful creations of the old masters, or make copies of these treasures, but are driven to create something of their own, to add their voice to a timeless symphony that resonates in the minds and visions of *rasikas*, to dip their *kalam* in their palette of new colours to re-create timeless forms, to pick new flowers and add a few petals of their own to Krishna's *vanamala* and not be just idle by-standers in the eternal *rasa lila* of Krishna, for even today they wish to become *gopis* and enter the *rasa mandala* and participate in the endless and timeless joy of celebrating Krishna's love by becoming Kanhapriya, or *gopis* beloved of Krishna, who wait under the Kadamba tree enchanted by the distant sounds of His flute.

Harsha V. Dehejia

THE POET AND THE PAINTERS OF KANHAPRIYA

Harsha V. Dehejia
Harsha V. Dehejia has a double doctorate, one in Medicine and the other in Ancient Indian Culture, both from Mumbai University. He is also a Member of the Royal College of Physicians of London and Glasgow and a Fellow of the Royal College of Physicians of Canada, all by examination. He is a practising Physician in Ottawa and also Adjunct Professor in the College of Humanities of Carleton University in Ottawa. His special interest in is Indian Aesthetics.

His publications include: Advaita of Art, Parvatidarpana, Despair and Modernity, Gods Beyond Temples and Leaves of a Pipal tree (all by Motilal Banarasidass, Delhi); Parvati: Goddess of Love, The Flute and The Lotus: Romantic Moments in Poetry and Painting and Celebrating Krishna: Sensuous Images, Sacred Words (all by Mapin, Ahmedabad); A Celebration of Love: The Romantic Heroine in the Indian Arts and A Festival of Krishna (both by Roli, Delhi).

"For me a journey from *kavya* to *kalam* in this Kanhapriya has been like going down a river like the blue-black Yamuna, the river that is dear to Krishna, the river that meanders through Vraj, singing and dancing, bringing to life well springs of love, carrying a whisper of the flute, inspiring and urging me to open my heart and mind to the love of Krishna, speaking in hushed voices of his *kridas* and *lilas*, inviting me to dip my hands into its limpid waters and take a sip, for in it I find his *madhurya*. Those of us who are touched by Krishna poetry and painting belong to the hallowed *parampara* of poets who have come before us, and every word that I write connects me to that illustrious pedigree of poets. For flowing through me are the words of Keshav and Bihari, Vidyapati and Ghanananda and many others. My thoughts are shaped by their well sculpted motifs and charged metaphors, my feelings are shaped by their ideas and images, my path has been lit by the light of their timeless creations. To say that I have created new poetry would be inappropriate if not a sacrilege, for the timeless love of Krishna and Radha flows through me as it has through trackless generations of poets and is being expressed through my words. I am a mere *bhakta* and participant in the eternal *lila* of Krishna's love."

Krishan Gopal Piyoosh Guleri
Krishan Gopal Piyoosh Guleri (born 1940) hails from the family of royal priests of the erstwhile Guler state. Dr Guleri writes both in Hindi and Himachali. He is a renowned writer and has done pioneering research on the noted writer Chandradhar Sharma Guleri. He retired as head of the department (Hindi) from the Post Graduate College in Dharamsala.

Shri Guleri has trans-created Harsha V. Dehejia's poetry from English into Brajbhasha.

In this portfolio we present compositions by contemporary artists. Led by Vijay Sharma of Chamba, who is a celebrated master artist, these artists from Rajasthan and Himachal have kept alive the traditions of miniature painting that originated in the ateliers of Rajput courts many centuries ago. It is as if the energy and inspiration of masters such as Sahibdin and Manohar, Nainsukh and Ranhja flows through their kalam, keeping alive a beautiful tradition of transforming kavya into chitra, so that the shringara rasa of Krishna is not only felt but seen, is not only contained in the throbbing of the heart but equally in the pleasure of the discerning eye.

Kailash Chand Sharma
Born in 1944 in Jaipur Kailash Chand Sharma hails from a family of traditional painters (mussawir). He ranks amongst the senior painters of Jaipur. He is an accomplished painter who works with ease on both paper and wall. Perhaps he is the only artist carrying on the painting tradition in Jaina style.

Vijay Sharma
Born in 1962 Vijay Sharma is an award winning Pahari miniaturist and works as an artist in the Bhuri Singh Museum, Chamba, Himachal Pradesh. He has studied major collections of Indian painting across the world and has held several exhibitions and lecture-demonstrations in leading museums and institutions in India and abroad. He has written several scholarly articles on Pahari miniature painting. He paints in various styles of Indian painting, chiefly Basohli and Kangra schools of Pahari painting. However, the work included here in Chaura-panchashika style reveals the fertile imagination of the artist.

Nathu Lal Verma
Born in 1946 Nathu Lal Verma is one of the foremost contemporary painters of Rajasthan and has been teaching art at the University of Rajasthan, Jaipur. A worthy disciple of late Kripal Singh Shekhawat, Verma has evolved his own style that exhibits a happy blend of traditional and contemporary trends. He is the recipient of the National Award from the Lalit Kala Academy and the All India Award from the Kalidas Akademi, Ujjain. Dr. Verma has been a senior fellow of the Department of Culture.

Hukam Chand Sharma
Born in 1968 in a Brahmin family of Jaipur Hukam Chgand Sharma is an accomplished painter, who paints with ease in the Mughal, Mewar and Kishangarh styles of Indian painting. His inquisitive mind and insatiable desire to learn the secrets of traditional pigments compelled him to pay several visits to Chamba where he was influenced by the master artist Vijay Sharma.

Parikshit Sharma
Born in 1978 Parikshit Sharma is a student and relative of Vijay Sharma of Chamba and works at the atelier of the latter. Parikshit is an artist of promise and follows the footsteps of his guru. He also paints in Basohli as well Guler-Kangra styles of Pahari painting. Recently, he was awarded the Himachal Sate award of excellence in painting.

Artist: Vijay Sharma

गैया को चरावत औ' खावत है नवनीत।
श्याम ग्वाल बाल संग अपरम्पार है।।
गोपियों का लूट लिया मन चितचोर ने।
उन के उरोजन में प्रेम का उभार है।।
कब लौटे सांवरा सलोना वृंदावन से।
नैनन में गोपियों के छिपा इंतजार है।।
अर्पण करने को ढेर सारा नवनी।
मानो मन मटकी में भरा हुआ प्यार है।।

Look at Krishna as he takes the cows to pasture
and at midday has his repast with the cowherds
when evening comes and the cows return home
the gopis wait expectantly for him
their day has gone in Krishna's absence
they wait with pots of milk and curd
as an offering to Krishna.

Artist: Kailash Chand Sharma

मन्दिर को जाती एक सखी दूजी सखी संग।
रास्ते में प्रेमभाव पूर्ण बतियाती है।।
प्रेम से जो दिया दीया रसिक रसीले को।
मन्दिर में भेंट करूं बात मन भाती है।।
दूसरी ने कहा-मेरा प्रिय है विदेश गया।
बार-बार मोहन की याद मुझे आती है।।
तभी मन भाता है सुहाती भेंट देने को।
रात को जो लिखी उसे मैंने प्रेम-पाती है।।

Two sakhis were walking towards a temple.

One sakhi asked the other
What will you offer at the temple?

I will offer a diya that I have made
I offered it first to my husband at home
for in that diya is my love.

And what will you offer at the temple
the sakhi asked her friend?
My beloved is away and I have no peace without him.

Why don't you make an offering of your love to Shivji
the friend asked.?

No, my love is only for my beloved.
I will offer my love letter to Shivji.

Artist: Hukam Chand Sharma

कहां रहता सांवला औ' कैसा है सुहाना रूप।
कहो सखी मैं हूं दिन रात इसी धुन में।।
पात-पात गाता गीत जहां है कदम्ब का।
पग-पग गोकुल कन्हैया रूप में उन में।।
जमुना तरंग व मयूर की उमंग में।
मधुर संगीत सुनो मुरली की धुन में।।
गैया-गैया सुरभि, चरैया मन मोहन,
फिर भी है राधा सखी! क्यूं उधेड़बुन में।।

One sakhi asked another
I have heard but not known about Krishna's love
Where does he stay and how do I get to see him?
The sakhi replied
where the kadmaba tree sings a song of love
where the parijatak whispers
the rhythms of love poetry
where the wind carries a sweet melody
where every tree becomes a Kalpavriksha
and every cow a Surabhi
where the dance of the peacock
the whispers of the bees
the songs of the birds and the message
of the Yamuna
teaches you a lesson of sweet love
there you will hear the sound of the flute
and it is there that you will meet Krishna.

Artist: Vijay Sharma

ध्यानरत ध्यानमग्न बोली एक गोपिका,
सखी प्रेम मग्न मेरा जीवन आकाश है।
झूम-झूम घूम-घूम पंछी के समान, कान्हा,
सान्ध्यकाल जैसे किसी आसन की आस है।
सत्ता सिंहासन सदा धूल के समान राधे!
महिमा, प्रताप, यश, गौरव भी त्रास है।
प्रेम पदमासन में बैठते हैं नित्य प्रेमी
जहां निराकार एकाकार का निवास है।

It was a spiritual moment in Vrindavana
and a gopi asked her sakhi

During the day my love is like a bird
its home is in the vast and boundless sky
but as twilight comes it needs a home to rest
it requires an asana where it can find comfort.

So they went to Krishna with their question.

Krishna said
A king sits on a throne for it is the symbol of power
and it speaks of his glory and majesty
but love needs no power nor glory
it is tender and soft, it should rest on a padmasana.
For in the padma there is a message
that love should be rooted in dharti
but spread in every direction to seek the radiance of the sun
and the light of the moon.

Artist: Hukam Chand Sharma

विस्मृति

बोली राधा मानिनी, सहेली! कहो कान्हा से।
मुझे भूल जाने का यह भाव कैसे आया था।।
कैसे भूले जल क्रीड़ा यमुना में साथ-साथ।
बाद में जो तूने खुद आलता लगाया था।।
मेरा प्यारा रूप था अनूप बना तेरे लिये।
चलता था साथ-साथ जैसे मेरा साया था।।
टांका था गुलाब तूने आप मेरे बालों में।
भूले कैसे उसे श्याम! तुझे बहुत भाया था।

A Manini Radha told her sakhi

Go and tell Krishna that he has
abandoned me
For when he was here he would paint
my feet red
And play with me in water
And put a flower in my hair.
Now he has gone away and does not
even care to visit me.

The sakhi went to Krishna and conveyed
this message to him.

स्मृति

हाय ! हाय !! सोच लिया कैसे, कहो राधा से।
मेरी प्यारी मानिनी, मैं कैसे भूल जाऊंगा।।
प्यार की उमंग छिपी जमुना तरंग में।
तेरे अंग-संग हूं मैं बार-बार आऊंगा।।
विकसित पारिजात फूल मेरे प्यार के।
तेरे प्रेम पगे शतदल बन भाऊंगा।।
मोर व चकोर संग सावन के बदरा।
बरस-बरस नाचूं तेरे संग गाऊंगा।।

Said Krishna to the sakhi

Please tell Radha that I am still with her
The lotuses that bloom in the Yamuna
have been coloured by me
and the yellow blossoms on the mango
tree have opened because of my love
and when peacocks dance and the clouds
of shravan pour rain
they do so because of my love
and when two birds sing to each other
they speak of my love for her.

In all of this is my love for Radha.

Artist: Vijay Sharma

राधा कहे, भले की है देवी की उपासना।
तब भी कन्हैया ने न सर्वस्व दिया है।।
उत्तर मे बोला मनमोहन तपाक से।
कदम्ब, पारिजात-रूप भोली तेरा पिया है।।
यमुना की लहर औ' भ्रमर की बहार में।
याद करो प्रेम अमृत कैसे पिया है।।
इनमें न पाई क्यूं न प्रेम विधि राधिके!
गोकुल की गली-गली ढूंढे तुझे जिया है।।

Radha said

I have worshiped the devi with appropriate rituals
and night and day I have loved Krishna
But why has Krishna not performed any sacraments of love?

Krishna replied

The fragrance of the parijatak
and the whispers of the leaves of the Kadamba tree
the rhythms of love in the dance of the peacock
the sweet talk of the bees
and the songs of love in the rain.
Did you not feel the sacraments of love in them?

Artist: Vijay Sharma

छोड़ गया फिर से एकान्त प्रेमी नायिका को।
दुखी मन नायिका का भोर की यह बेला है।।
गयी थी सहेली संग, बाल कमलताल में।
लगा हुआ देखा वहां पक्षियों का मेला है।।
पोत दिया पीत था कबूतरी को चंदन से।
छोड़ उसे उड़ा तभी पक्षियों का रेला है।।
मन को मसोस कर सोचती थी घड़ी-घड़ी।
काल गाल व्याल रूप जीवन अकेला है।।

When after an amorous night the morning sun appeared
The nayaka left leaving the nayika by herself
she felt forsaken and lonely and looked
two pigeons were sporting near the lotus pond
she dipped her hand in sandalwood paste and camphor
and applied it to a pigeon and coloured it yellow
the mate not recognising it any more, flew away
leaving the nayika and the yellow pigeon to share their loneliness.

Artist: Vijay Sharma

विरह में दग्ध-विदग्ध हाय! नायिका।
दुखी मन कदम्ब की ओट लिए खड़ी है।।
ऐसे क्यों हो खड़ी पूछा उसे एक सखी ने।
नैनन में क्यूं यह तेरे आंसुओं की झड़ी है।।
प्रेम-अमृत मिला उन्हें क्या मालूम सखी।
विरह के दुख की बड़ी अजीब लड़ी है।।
गिरा पात-पात को समेट बोली गोद में।
सखी यह आशीष मिली, बड़ी शुभ घड़ी है।।

A Virahini nayika stood holding the branch of a tree
as a lata wound around the trunk
two pigeons sported underneath
and two parrots on the branch above
whispered to each other
and peacocks performed a dance of love.
Her sakhi asked why do you stand thus?
Said the nayika
The pleasures of love are for all to see
the pain of love is only for those who know.
As she said this a leaf fell from the tree into her odhni
and she felt blessed.

Artist: Vijay Sharma

पिया बोला नायिका से जानो मेरी मानिनी।
दोनों का यह नाम, रूप कविता संगीत है।।
झूम-झूम झूमता जो कमल पे भौंरा।
छिपा हुआ इसी में हमारा प्रेम गीत है।।
बरखा फुहार में मयूर का यह नाचना।
धरा की सुगंध सौंधी, अपनी ही जीत है।।
पहाड़ी चित्रकला में निहारती जो नायिका।
लगे मुझे भाव में विभोर मेरा गीत है।।

Yesterday you said that I had written our names together
but doesn't every love poem carry our names?
And when two birds are sitting together on a branch
are they not you and me?
And when black bees are attracted to a lotus
are they not carrying a message from me to you?
When maples bring forth their pink blossoms in the spring
are they not whispering of our love?
And when tulips spring up after their long slumber
and a yellow flower grows besides a red
is it not the two of us holding hands?
And when the rains are about to come
and the peacock dances with joy
is that not our song that is being sung?
Ans when the first drops of rain fall on the earth
and there is the fragrance of the wet soil
is that not the aroma of our love?
And when in a Pahadi painting
a nayak looks longingly at a nayika
is it not my gaze and your beauty that are being depicted?
Tell me, premika is not our name in every love song?

Artist: Nathu Lal Verma

कर रही सोलह श्रृंगार राधा रानी जब।
इतने में चुपके से श्याम वहां आ गये।।
टांक दिया फूल पारिजात घने बालों में।
रूप था अनूप श्याम राधा-मन भा गये।।
राधा हुई सांवली कन्हैया गोरे राधा सम।
एक-नेक हुए दोनों प्रेम-गान गा गए।।
प्रेम में यह लीला हाव था महान वंदना।
द्वैत भाव मिटा, आनन्दब्रह्म पा गए।।

Let me show you an enchanting sight
Radha is adorning herself with the help of her sakhis
all the sixteen adornments were looking radiant on her body
but still her mind was in a state of longing.
Just then Krishna appeared and placed a parijat flower in her hair.
When Radha saw her face in the mirror she was radiant
now her adornment was complete.
Krishna said my beloved you and I are one
you are me and I am you.
It has been rightly said that the lane of love is so narrow
that it does not have place for two.
Love cannot sustain dvaita, only a pure advaita.

Artist: Vijay Sharma

पूछा जब घूम कर प्रेमिका ने प्रेमी से।
कहो कैसे सदा प्रेम पूत रह पायेगा।।
नायक ने कहा कर धरती की वंदना।
इसी स्थल कल्प वृक्ष स्वयं उग आएगा।।
उमड़-उमड़ घुमड़-घुमड़ सांवला सलोना मेघ।
प्यार का अमिय झूम-झूम बरसायेगा।।
डाल-डाल पात-पात गुल्म-गुल्म बैठकर।
झुंड-झुंड पक्षियों का प्रेमगीत गायेगा।।

A nayaka asks the nayika

Who will inherit our love, a love that is so pure?
Touching the earth the nayaka said
it is the earth, that will inherit our love
from it will rise a kalpavriksha
on which will sit birds who will sing a song of our love
and when the wind blows through it will
whisper softly of our romance
and when lovers sit underneath it
they will speak in hushed voices of our love
and when rains falls on the tree
it will gently bring with it our blessings
that all love should be as pure and ever lasting as ours.

Artist: Vijay Sharma

गोपिका नवेलियां सातों सहेलियां,
ठुमक-ठुमक नृत्यमय पनघट को जा रहीं।
हास, लास, रास-रंग रंजित थीं गोपियां,
गायन के सात सुरों जैसी थी सुहा रहीं।
उमड़-उमड़ घुमड़ उठे मस्तमन मेघ तब,
सुरभि संगीत सम सुरमई थी भा रहीं।
सुन्दर बहार संग बरखा फुहार थी,
मेघ मल्हार मानो राग सभी गा रहीं।

Seven gopis were going to fetch water
and they seemed like seven musical notes
and when they heard the flute of Krishna
they mingled with the clouds
and when it rained
one heard raga megha malhar.

चित्रकार- कैलाशचन्द शर्मा जयपुर।
२००७

HUKAM CHAND SHARMA

Vijay

Vijay

नाथूलाल
०८